W9-COU-986

Me + 1D!

First published by Parragon in 2013
Parragon
Chartist House
15–17 Trim Street
Bath BA1 1HA, UK
www.parragon.com

Cover photos: Getty Images, Rex Features
Internal photos: FilmMagic, Getty Images, iStockphoto,
MCT via Getty Images, Press Association, Rex Features,
WireImage

ISBN 978-1-4723-1071-2

Printed in China

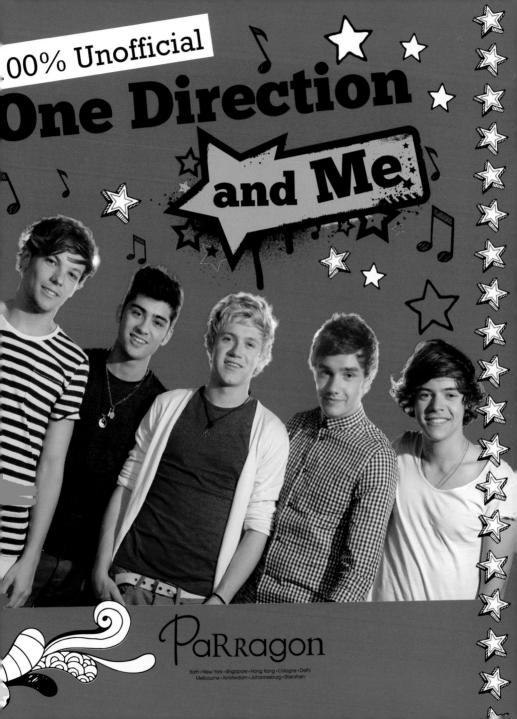

Contents

One Direction

We Want 1D

Hey Directioners, welcome to 1DHQ!

Pick up your backstage pass and come inside for all the gossip about the ama**ZAYN**, fabu**LOUIS**, extraordin**HARRY**, bril**LIAM**, phenome**NIALL** ... ONE DIRECTION!

Liam James Payne
Nickname: Paynee
Born: August 29, 1993
Liam's luck: Liam was first in *The X Factor* when he was just 14 and made it through to Judges' Houses, but Simon Cowell felt he was too young at the time. Lucky for us, he tried again in 2010—and ended up in One Direction!

Harry Edward Styles
Nickname: Hazza or H
Born: February 1, 1994
Styles' secret: Before he auditioned for *The X Factor*, Harry was in his own band, White Eskimo, with some friends.

Louis William Tomlinson
Nickname: Lou or Boo Bear
Born: December 24, 1991
Tomlinson's truth: Louis is a big joker. When he played Danny Zuko in his school production of *Grease*, he mooned the audience ... And the principal was watching!

Zayn Jawaad Malik
Nickname: Zaynster
Born: January 12, 1993
Zayn's pain: Zayn is a super-tidy person, so when he shared a room with messy Louis and Harry in the X Factor house, they drove him crazy!

Niall James Horan
Nickname: Nialler
Born: September 13, 1993
Niall's file: Niall was a star from the start. While lining up for his X Factor audition, he caught the attention of the crowd by playing his guitar and singing Justin Bieber's "One Time"!

All About Me

Write your name here

....

is the number one Directioner ever!

I am _____ years old.

My catchphrase is _____.

_____

My fave hobby is _____

_____

My bestie is _____

_____

My fave member of 1D is _____

_____

The three words I would use to describe him are

_____

_____

_____ .

_____

Zayn rocks!

Stick your best 1D pic or a photo of you at their concert here

I ♥ Niall!

I am One Direction's biggest fan because

_____.

What I would say if I met …

Liam: _____.

Harry: _____.

Zayn: _____.

Niall: _____.

Louis: _____.

The present I would give to my fave band member is _____.

Louis love!

My 1D concert banner would look like this:

Me + 1D!

Mrs. Styles!

Supercute Liam!

1D Mania

From ordinary boys to one of the world's biggest boy bands ... here ar the fab five's 5 Steps to Success!

1 School Daze

The 1D boys have always been into music. Liam wer to a performing arts group. Harry won a battle of the bands competition with his band, White Eskimo. Nial was in a choir and won a local singing competition. Zayn sang in the school choir and loved acting, too. Louis was in a band called The Rogue and put on shows at school.

2 Xtra Special

Then came *The X Factor* ... In 2010, the boys auditioned as solo acts. They were shaking with nerves, but they all made it through to Bootcamp. The boys performed well, but the judges couldn't see them as solo acts, and they were all sent home.

3

One Direction Detection

It wasn't over! The boys were asked if they wanted to form a band, and they all said "yes!" Simon Cowell became their mentor, and they made it through to *The X Factor* final. But when the winning act was announced ... it wasn't One Direction. The boys came in third.

4

It's a Sign

The boys wanted to stay together as a band and were over the moon when Simon Cowell revealed that he was signing them! After that, nothing could stop them. Their first single, "What Makes You Beautiful," went straight to number one in the U.K.!

5

1D Mania Arrives!

With the 1D fans behind them, the boys went from strength to strength. Their first U.K. tour sold out in minutes. They won the Best British Single at the 2012 BRIT Awards. And it wasn't just the U.K. that loved them ... soon the whole world caught 1D Mania!

All they want is to continue to grow and experience everything they can ... and they want you to come with them!

Liam

The daddy of the group!

Liam says that he's serious "23½/7"! But that's because being a singer means so much to him, and he doesn't want to mess anything up.

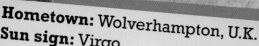

Hometown: Wolverhampton, U.K.
Sun sign: Virgo
Height: 5'10"
Eye color: Brown
Family: Two older sisters named Nicola and Ruth

Liam's faves

School subjects: Science and PE
Color: Purple
Childhood memory: Going to Disneyland
And: Girls with curly hair!

We ♥ Liam!

☆ Liam started singing karaoke when he was just six years old! His favorite song to perform was Robbie Williams' "Angels."
☆ At one time, Liam wanted to be a boxer, but he gave it up for *The X Factor* because he couldn't turn up on stage with bruises!
☆ Liam used to make money by buying boxes of candy and selling them at school for a profit. He made $75 a week!

Zayn on Liam …

Zayn thinks being in One Direction is good for Liam—the other guys have helped him to be more immature!

If he wasn't in One Direction, he might be …

Working at the same factory as his dad, building airplanes. He thought it would be like playing with giant Lego!

Which Liam Do You ♥ Best?

Liam changes his look more often than Niall changes polo shirts! What's your favorite style for Mr. Payne?

Start here and follow the arrows.

Chill out or dress up?

dress up

chill out

Movies or shopping?

shopping

movies

Sign off with ☺ or sign off with 'xo'?

☺

xo

Skateboarding or in-line skating?

skating

Music or sports?

music

sports

Night

boarding

Liam's long hair or Liam's short 'do?

short

"Live While We're Young" or "Up All Night"?

Young

long

Go to a movie premiere or music awards?

premiere

awards

Boys in jeans or boys in suits?

jeans

suits

Cool 'n' Sporty

Smart 'n' Swag

Totally Trendy

15

Harry

The flirt of the group!

Harry was mischievous at school—no surprises there! He always had lots of friends and had his first real girlfriend when he was 12.

Hometown: Holmes Chapel, Cheshire, U.K
Sun sign: Aquarius
Height: 5'10"
Eye color: Green/blue
Family: One older sister named Gemma

Harry's faves

Color: Orange
TV show: *Family Guy*
School subjects: English and Drama
And: Girls with short hair!

ALL ARE

Harry's got style!

☆ Harry played badminton a lot in high school. He liked that it was an unusual sport and required a lot of skill.

☆ Harry is really sweet and takes care of his friends from before he was famous. He even organized for one friend to get work experience on the 1D tour!

Liam on Harry ...

Liam says it must be really weird for Harry, because girls go crazy for him!

If he wasn't in One Direction, he might be ...

Working his Saturday job in a bakery and going to college.

Harry's Name Game

Do you and Mr. Styles have something secret in common? Find out using your Directionumber!

To figure out a Directionumber, use the letters from a first name. Take, for example, HARRY.

Count out where each letter of the name sits in the alphabet. A = 1, B = 2, C = 3, and so on.

H = 8, A = 1, R = 18, R = 18, Y = 25

Now add all of those numbers together.

8 + 1 + 18 + 18 + 25 = 70

Finally, keep adding the digits of the total number until you're left with one single number.

7 + 0 = 7

Write your number here.

Harry's Directionumber is 7. What's yours?

_____

Do you have a Directioner match with Harry?
Try it with all of the boys' names—and for your friends, too!

Niall

The joker of the group!
Niall loves to laugh. He always talked at school, and he's the biggest chatterbox in the group!

Hometown: Mullingar in Westmeath, Ireland
Sun sign: Virgo
Height: 5'7"
Eye color: Blue
Family: An older brother named Greg

Niall's faves
Color: Blue
Food: Spaghetti
School subjects: French and Geography
And: Funny girls with dimples!

Harry on Niall ...
Harry says that the boys all have funny rhyming names for each other, and Niall has a few ... "Kyle," "Kitchen Tile," and "Nail File"!

Niall's cool factor
☆ When Niall was nine, he played Oliver in the school play. It gave him a taste of how great it felt to perform for an audience.
☆ Niall can speak Spanish really well! It came in handy for ordering pizza when they were in Spain for Judges' Houses.

If he wasn't in One Direction, he might be ...
At college studying sound engineering.

Niall's Superstar Search

How well do you know 1D's Irish cutie? Fill in the answers, then find those words in the grid. Look forward, backward, up, down, and diagonally.

Niall's best ever Christmas present was his _ _ _ _ _ _.

His first pets were two goldfish named Tom and _ _ _ _ _.

Niall is friends with superstar singer, Justin _ _ _ _ _ _.

4. The bird that Niall is scared of is the _ _ _ _ _ _.

Niall's biggest idol is the singer Michael _ _ _ _ _.

When Niall was young, he had an imaginary friend named _ _ _ _ _ _ _.

7. Niall would like to be tall, like his fave animal the _ _ _ _ _ _ _.

8. Niall's totally weird mascot is a pair of white _ _ _ _ _.

```
N R U K X C C U A Q P U
A E F F A R I G K J T J
R A R D F Y M O X F T B
C V V G U I T A R L U B
I K C D H P A N S B Q O
S F B E L H U C L Q Y Z
S A L Z E I E E H B S N
U B U I A Y S W X T G D
S I E L H O H Y A C I N
J E B J C Z D P R Y Y Y
R B E E I B S Y R R U U
U E L A M K K I Q F E I
S R L I C B S I G O Q J
Q Y H O G O H D R V L R
G V S Y N O E G I P D Q
```

1. guitar, 2. Jerry, 3. Bieber, 4. pigeon, 5. Bublé, 6. Michael, 7. giraffe, 8. socks.

Zayn

The stylish one of the group!

Zayn may seem quiet at times, but only because the other boys are so loud! He describes himself as just a bit shy and awkward.

Zayn's faves

Color: Red
Childhood memory: Going to the fair with his mom and grandma
And: Naturally pretty girls that he can spoil!

Hometown: East Bowling, Bradford, U.K.
Sun sign: Capricorn
Height: 5'9"
Eye color: Brown
Family: An older sister named Doniya and two younger sisters named Waliyha and Safaa

Niall on Zayn ...

Niall says that Zayn was the most nervous about dancing, but now he's really good at it!

If he wasn't in 1D, he might be ...

Studying to be an actor or drama teacher.

Stuff about Zayn

☆ Zayn has always been pretty spoiled because he's the only boy in his family.
☆ He has acted since he was 12 and played Bugsy in *Bugsy Malone*. He was also in *Scrooge* and *Grease* at school.
☆ He hid backstage during *The X Factor* Bootcamp choreography

Zayn's Fact or Faked?

Vas happenin', Directioners? Can you guess which of these ridic' rumors about Zayn are real and which are totally made up?

1. Zayn hurt his ankle at Justin Bieber's house after the VMAs.

2. Zayn cries at chick flicks.

3. Zayn thinks babies and animals are really scary.

4. Zayn draws funny cartoons of the other guys when they're hanging out.

5. Zayn says the 1D boys have their own coded sign language.

6. Zayn had to stand on top of a brick to be tall enough for his first kiss.

7. Zayn has always been really confident.

8. Zayn's sisters helped him to write his first love letter to a girl at school.

Answers: 1. True, 2. True, 3. False: he loves them and says they make him go all gooey, 4. True, 5. False, but they do have secret words that nobody else understands, 6. True, 7. False: he was really shy before he went on The X Factor, 8. True.

Louis

The prankster of the group!

Louis loved school, simply because he got to see his friends. He was always the one doing silly stuff to make people laugh.

Hometown: Doncaster, U.K.
Sun sign: Capricorn
Height: 5'9"
Eye color: Blue
Family: Four younger sisters named Lottie, Fizzy, and twins Daisy and Phoebe

Louis' faves

Food to cook: He doesn't really cook, so he makes cereal!
Color: Red
Movie: *Grease*
And: Chatty girls who don't wear too much makeup!

Louis' best stuff

☆ Being the eldest in the band, Louis is the one who takes care of most of the official stuff, like emails and calls from management.
☆ He says he's always been a bit "gabby." Even when he was a toddler in his stroller he would talk to people he didn't know!

If he wasn't in 1D, he might be …

Studying to be a drama teacher. He and Zayn might have been on the same course!

Niall on Louis …

When they first formed the band, Niall suggested they all dress like Louis, because he thought he looked so cool!

Louis' Secret Message

Louis has something funny to tell you ... but you've got to figure out what it is! Translate the special Directioner message using the 1D code.

What's Your 1D IQ?

Try this 1D super-fan quiz to find out!

Which bandmate?

1 Which bandmate supposedly has smelly feet, because he doesn't wear socks?

_____

2 Who always wears two pairs of socks?

_____

3 Who is great at doing accents?

_____

4 Who had a man crush on Taylor Lautner?

_____

5 Who likes to spend his time off chillaxing on the couch?

_____

6 What's the first thing Liam said he would do if he were Simon Cowell for a day?

A Create a new girl band

B Buy a bouncy castle

C Wear a suit made of money

7 What unusual fans did Niall say he wanted th band to have in 10 yea

A Grannies

B Animals

C Aliens

8 What kind of animal did Liam buy as a present for his family?

A A pet tarantula

B A Labrador puppy

C A lop-eared rabbit

9 What part of his One Direction doll did Louis ask to be redone because he thought it looked bad?

A His clothes

B His hair

C His nose

10 Which famous singer put Niall through to the next round on *The X Factor*?

A Katy Perry

B Nicole Scherzinger

C Rihanna

How did you do?

1–3 correct	4–7 correct	8–10 correct
Directioner in training, who will be a number one fan of the future.	Devoted Directioner, who can be an expert with a little more reading.	Directioner diva, who would pass every 1D test!

1D's New Bandmate!

(Okay, so he's made up

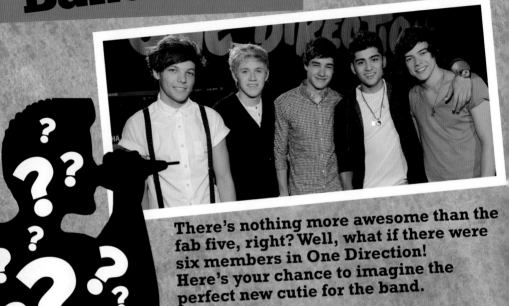

There's nothing more awesome than the fab five, right? Well, what if there were six members in One Direction! Here's your chance to imagine the perfect new cutie for the band.

My new member would be named _____

Pick a 1D member for each of the lines below:

He would have hair like _____

He would have _____'s fashion sense.

He would have a voice like _____

He would have _____'s sense of humor.

His best friend in the band would be _____

26

Sixth Member Stuff!

Nickname: _____

Catchphrase: _____

Fave song: _____

Fave color: _____

Biggest secret: _____

Design an outfit for your new bandmate! Don't forget to add funky accessories.

Autograph:

_____

27

Got to Gossip!

Check out some of the most
1-derful secrets about
your fave boys ever!

The Name Game

How did One Direction come up with their band name? Did they spend hours throwing around different ideas? No—it was the first name they came up with! Harry thought of it because they were all moving in the same direction as a group.

Prank-tastic

The 1D boys have real boys' humor. Sometimes they'll play a word game where they have to say random words while they're on stage—even if that means fitting them into the middle of songs!

A Touch of Magic

aniel Radcliffe, a.k.a. Harry otter, was one of the band's biggest supporters when they were on *The X Factor*. And at some stage or other, all of the boys have had a crush on Emma Watson, who plays Hermione!

Dating Disaster

Liam's first crush was a girl named Emily. When he finally worked up the courage to ask her out, he found her by the school lockers and sang to her. She dumped him the next day! Awwww.

Keeping Cool

Liam is secretly really clumsy! Once, at a book signing, he slurped a bottle of soda too fast, so it bubbled over and spilled all over him.

Let's Dance

The boys get a little embarrassed when they practice new dance moves, so they made a deal not to tease each other!

Crazy Quotes!

1 "I'm an emotional guy, so I don't have to worry about a girl trying to get me to open up."

2 "Signing my first autograph was quite awkward because I didn't have one."

3 "Live fast, have fun, and be a bit mischievous."

4 "Whenever I'm sad, I just imagine babies with moustaches."

5 "One time, Niall sat on the floor for hours trying to find a way of putting his M&Ms in alphabetical order."

6 "No matter how many time people try to criticize you, the best revenge is to prove them wrong."

7 "I think there is nothing wrong with eating all the time. At least I'm not doing anything illegal."

8 "We went to a farm and they offered us horses to ride. There were only four horses so Harry rode a cow."

9 "Just because you have flaws does not mean you aren't beautiful."

10 "Until I find the perfect girl, I have Louis."

30

Answers: 1. Niall, 2. Harry 3. Louis, 4. Liam, 5. Louis, 6. Zayn, 7. Niall, 8. Liam, 9. Zayn, 10. Harry.

A Day in the Life of 1D

The One Direction boys went from normal guys to superstars in the blink of an eye. How have their lives changed? Well, here's what a typical day might look like for them now ...

8:00 a.m. Meeting fans
Harry greets some Directioners to sign stuff. The boys say they'll never complain about signing, because they do everything for their fans.

9:30 a.m. Getting around
Traveling is a part of the boys' life now, and these days they can do it in style! Check out this helicopter, which they used for flying around to promote a single.

11:00 a.m. Doing interviews
This is when being in a band is really helpful—there are five people to answer questions. But 1D are so full of energy, it's more about trying to get a word in!

2:30 p.m. Celeb signings

Book and CD signings are a great chance to talk to fans. Sometimes Directioners will even bring the band presents. Harry once said he liked turtles and ended up being given lots of turtle stuff.

:00 p.m. Walking the red carpet

D know how to work the red carpet n style. They look like a classic boy band in matching suits! Wonder who took the longest to do his hair!

7:30 p.m. Performing on stage

One Direction do what they do best! This is what it's all about—getting in front of the fans and belting out their biggest hits.

My One Direction Predictions

Get your crystal ball out, because it's time to take a sneak peek into the future! The 1D boys have already had a magical time, but what else do you think is in store for the fab five?

And the winner is …

Which boy would you predict for each of these wacky awards?

Most likely to write a song for the band: _____.

Most likely to grow a moustache: _____.

Least likely to learn to breakdance: _____.

Most likely to star in a movie: _____.

Least likely to write a book: _____.

Tomorrow's headlines

Can you complete these silly headline predictions?

Harry Gets Head Stuck in a _____

One Direction Buy a Big _____ **to Live In**

Liam Reveals New Pet _____

Niall Asks _____ **to Join One Direction!**

Which 1D Boy is 4U?

Who is your favorite band member? And what does your choice say about you?

Liam

You're a dependable friend and like to look after everyone around you.
Lucky color: Blue
Special symbol: Smiley face

Harry

You're honest and really fun to be around, so you're never short of friends.
Lucky color: Red
Special symbol: Heart

Niall

You're fun and full of energy, and great at making people laugh.
Lucky color: Green
Special symbol: Clover

Zayn

You're sweet and caring, and really good at helping others with their problems.
Lucky color: Purple
Special symbol: Lightning bolt

Louis

You're a real performer and always keep people entertained.
Lucky color: Yellow
Special symbol: Star

What's Your 1D Song Match?

Which One Direc[tion] song would the b[oys] sing for you? Find out in this fun quiz!

Start here and follow the arrows.

Are you a good singer?

no → Have you been to see 1D in concert?

yes ↓ Do you follow @onedirection on Twitter?

yes — Have you been to see 1D in concert? → yes

no → Do you have a crush on one of the boys?

Do you follow @onedirection on Twitter? — no → Do you have a crush on one of the boys?

yes ↓

yes → Do you know the words to all of One Direction's songs?

Do you have a crush on one of the boys? → ye[s]

Do you like dance tunes better than ballads? yes

no →

Do you know the words to all of One Direction's songs? no → Do you like dance tunes better than ballads?

36

Have you been a fan since they were on *The X Factor*?

no

"One Thing"
You love laughing with your friends, just like the boys do in this video. You're crazy fun and love to dance!

yes

"What Makes You Beautiful"
You love this song because it reminds you of when 1D were just getting famous. You're friendly, loyal, and love to giggle.

no

Do you have any of the boys' names scribbled on your schoolbooks?

yes

"Gotta Be You"
You love singing along to slow ballads, and this is one of your all-time faves. You're sweet, sensitive, and the perfect bestie.

yes

Do you have a 1D poster in your bedroom?

no

37

Be Part of Team 1D

One Direction has a whole bunch of helpers that make them look supercool and sound their best. And these lucky people get to hang out with the boys all day! What special skill could you bring to the 1D team?

Be 1D's songwriter

Are you good at writing stories or poems? These could be lyrics! Harry and the boys have cowritten a number of their songs, and Niall is amazing on the guitar, but they still need the help of experts like you!

 Write your first-ever 1D chorus here:

Be 1D's photographer

Maybe you're great at taking photos of you and your friends ... Sneak pics of the boys while they're hanging out, and take their official photos for their album covers. This is the perfect job for you!

Be 1D's stylist

It's a full-time job keeping up with Liam's hairstyles alone! Would you enjoy picking outfits for the boys? Could you look after the wardrobe of Harry's bow ties and Louis' suspenders?

Design a new outfit for your fave band member here.

Be 1D's choreographer

Are you a great dancer? One Direction may not be into dance routines, but they still need someone to show them how to move around the stage. If you'd love hanging out stage-side and on set, then this is the job for you!

So what's the ideal job for you?

Backstage with 1D

Want to know what the One Direction boys are up to when we can't see them? Take a peek at some of the behind-the-scenes antics ...

Louis is totally accident prone!

Louis' joking around can sometimes land him in trouble. Remember when he ended up in the hospital during Judges' Houses in *The X Factor*? He was messing around in the ocean and got stung by a sea urchin. In the morning, the sore foot was twice the size of the other one!

Harry and Louis have a bromance!

The Directioners call them "Larry Stylinson" because they're always together. Harry says he clicked with Louis from the start and feels like he can tell him anything, and Louis says Harry is his best friend. They live together and go on vacations together, too!

Zayn is addicted to his Nintendo DS™!

But that's not all—he's got a really creative side, too. He loves painting and drawing, and likes to do stuff for the 1D website. He also really likes writing poetry, so he's excited about working on more song ideas.

Liam has a phobia of spoons!

Weird, but true. When Liam's in a restaurant and doesn't know where a spoon has been, he can't use it! He's fine with all other kinds of silverware, though!

Ssssh!

Even though Zayn's famous now, he still likes to go to the supermarket with his mom. One time, to avoid getting recognized, he wore a hat and glasses as a disguise!

Oops!

Liam's pants have ripped while he's been on stage—twice!

Niall has a never-ending supply of polo shirts!

The other boys love teasing Niall about his polo shirt obsession. He's got them in just about every color imaginable.

41

What Did You Say?

Check out these funny pics of the 1D boys messing around. Add a funny caption with what they might be saying!

Do You Have 1D Mania?

Just how crazy are you about the One Direction boys? Answer the questions, then add up your answers to get your fan status.

What would you do if ...

1 ... you were going to a 1D book signing?
a. Just turn up on the day
b. Spend hours choosing an outfit and practicing hairstyles
c. Paint your face with "I ♥ 1D" and bring each of them the perfect present

2 ... you met your fave 1D boy while shopping with your mom?
a. Wander over and say hello
b. Hide! You're not wearing your fave outfit, and your mom will embarrass you!
c. Scream and push past everyone to get a pic on your phone.

4 ... you were given a backstage pass to a 1D concert?
a. Think it's really cool and pick a best friend to bring with you
b. Tell all of your friends— they're going to be super jealous!
c. Try ... to ... breathe! This is the most exciting thing ever.

3 ... you could snoop on their tour bus?
a. Look at where they hang out
b. Check out their wardrobe
c. Keep anything you find!

5 ... one of the 1D boys followed you on Twitter?
a. Get excited—now they'll know all the cool stuff you're doing
b. Spend ages thinking up cool tweets that will impress them
c. Tweet every day to tell them you're their number one fan!

6 1D night with friends

a. Checking out their latest clips on YouTube

b. Watching their videos over and over

c. Listening to their tunes and dancing around the room like crazy

7 1D X Factor song

a. Rihanna's "Only Girl in the World"

b. Coldplay's "Viva La Vida"

c. Kim Wilde's "Kids in America"

9 Singer that you'd love them to work with

a. Jessie J.

b. Selena Gomez

c. Justin Bieber

8 Way to meet One Direction

a. Without planning it—you just bump into them and get your pic taken

b. At a movie premiere by the red carpet— they come and sign your CD

c. At their concert—you and your friends are at the front and they touch your hands

Mostly a: One Direction Cool!

You're pretty chilled out, but that doesn't mean you're not a devoted Directioner! The boys would see you like one of their friends.

Mostly b: One Direction Crazy!

When it comes to 1D, you're out to impress! The boys would think you're supercool and a loyal Directioner.

Mostly c: One Direction Obsession!

There's no doubt about it … you've got 1D Mania! You'll be a true Directioner forever.